WHEN A MIND EXPLODES

WHEN A MIND EXPLODES

DEDA

I will go under the sheets with words.

I will birth poems

without the fear of being left behind,

for if I have learnt anything,

it is;

Poetry never abandons

the poet.

For all the overthinkers, the anxiety-stricken, the heartbroken, the ones who cannot seem to understand themselves, the ones who want to claw themselves out their own skin and mind,

this is for you,
for us.

Ps. We are going to be fine.

CONTENTS

THE
WILTING

When A Mind Explodes

And sometimes I wonder
if my whole life will be spent
putting myself together
and learning
how to breathe.

They say we should be happier
have a more positive outlook
stop thinking negatively.

As if it is that simple.
As if we see two paths
and choose the rougher one.

As if we wake up every day and say
to hell with happiness,
i wanna be freakin' depressed,
i wanna be anxiety-stricken.

As if
if someone could just
simply choose to live
a happier life
they'd even think of ending theirs.

If people could just choose
how they wanted to feel
everyone in the world would be elated.

~ *and here I was thinking that was a given*

When i say i'm tired
i hope they read in between the lines and see

---

tired of living in this mind and not being able
to escape

tired of fighting for each breath when all i want
to do is stop breathing

---

tired of waking up and living the same
torturous days on repeat

---

tired of wanting to let go but not
knowing how.

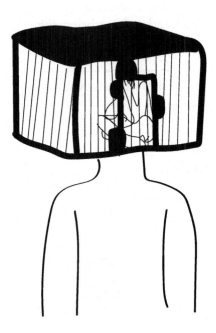

When your mind is the prison
there is no real escape
unless you lose your mind
but…

not unless.

A house is a dangerous thing

if it is not a home

and so can be ones mind.

I crave a silence so deafening
i cannot hear the thoughts
wreaking havoc in my head.

I am sorry that I'm not good at living in the moment,
at making good memories.
I am sorry I'm afraid of being too happy,
but it has always been the brightest moments
that created the darkest memories.

Uncertain if my joy
is genuine anymore

the line between
pretending and
feeling true happiness
has become so blurred

this is the result
of placing the heavy burden
of always being a bundle of joy
upon yourself

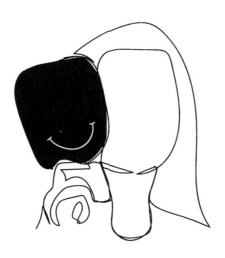

Some days i can't help but reminisce,
my hands find their way to the places
you've last touched,
wishing it were yours,
the bitter-sweet
burning sensation
you left behind
holding me captive,
driving me
crazy.

Sometimes I have no control
over whether my head or my heart
is on my body,
and what a lethal thing the latter
can be.

They ask me
why I have to be this way;
so difficult
so "full of attitude"

they never ask
if there was something bothering me
if I had burdens I needed help to carry

they always ask all
the wrong questions
and never the ones
that matter the most.

"feel", they said
and the tears meant
to cleanse me
drowned me
instead.

Barely anyone
speaks about
the dark side of love

how it callously stays
even when they leave

how it sometimes
feels like drowning.

if you leave tea out long enough
it will cool

and the sun always sets at the end
of each day

so I don't know why I thought
your warmth would have been
a permanent part of me.

It's somewhere between
a runny nose and a wet pillowcase
we realize that the one who
breaks a heart is seldom
the one to fix it,
we realize that if we ever
want to be happy again,
we must learn the art of mending ourselves.

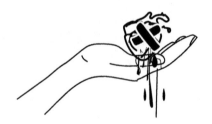

Deda

stolen hearts

left with spades

our love

nothing but

a cheated card game.

isn't it funny
how much our
eyes bleed

when it's our
hearts that are
wounded.

All I remember from
that day

is pain

heart wrenching
gut churning
wanting so badly to die
blinding pain

that still has me
unable to see
a way out
or a light I could follow
to healing.

When A Mind Explodes

I kept it all
in a cute little box

that eventually decayed
leaving toxins to float within me

that cute little box
I packed everything in

ended up
killing me.

Why does the trauma fasten
our lips instead
of opening them?

Why does all the courage our mothers
passed down condense into sweat
the moment we decide to
free ourselves from their
grasp?

I think it is because
society has made it so hard
for us to believe that we can be
our own saviors.

~ *but we can*

You wrought
a pleasant intoxication
kind of madness
in me

- change decided to be inevitable at the worst time –

you just had to
wrench it out
in a way so fierce
the butterflies turned
into vultures in my belly

everything sweet
turned sour

everything fruitful
turned into something
they could feast on.

You say I should let people in.
As if I haven't already been
host to enough

in the end, all they did
was leave,
dragging along with them
fragments of my being

i will not make the same mistake again
not when there is barely
anything left of me.

if I did something to deserve this
it must have been the most
vile, evil thing

so tell me
so that the guilt of it
may lessen the blow of this
awful reality I'm living.

Deda

What
inescapable
anguish
loving
the
wrong
person
a
little
too
much
kindles

If
only
apologies
held
the
power
to
heal
wounded
hearts

are you familiar with the agony
when the source of your happiness
is the very source of your pain
yet your heart refuses to be
set free from it?

i wish i was numb
at least then I wouldn't be able to feel…..

…… feeling deeply
leads to thinking deeply….

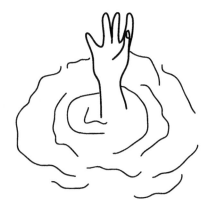

….. and thinking deeply
leads to drowning.

You masked your malevolence
with an impressive act of kindness

realization dawned
too late

i only ever noticed your intent
to dim my light
when it was completely
snuffed out.

Time only heals
if it is not spent thinking about you

and seldom is that the case.

My words have always been about you.
The way you loved me
the way you left
the way i'm aching without you.

I should have opened my eyes
to watch you leave
perhaps it would be easier
to remember you as
"the bad guy that left"
rather than the
"great guy I lost"

Even the shower is my enemy now.
the water's caress reminds me of you.
can't tell my tears from the droplets.
where are you now
when I need you
the most?

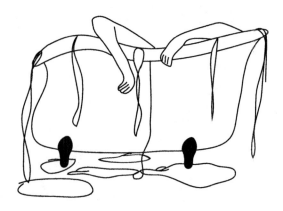

Deda

How fortunate it would be
if we could use the hurt people
caused us to melt away our love for them,

no matter how strong
the hurt will cause it to face death

no matter how confused you are,
one thing will be clear:

they hurt you
and
you don't love them anymore.

The only thing that hurt more than the lies
was that you didn't even think I was worthy of the truth.

Deda

The thoughts of you
cause my wounds to fester
and my heart to flatter
and experiencing both
simultaneously
is such a dangerous thing.

I loved you because I saw the pain
they inflicted upon you,
how the multiple stabs to your back
rendered you unable to walk away.

I loved you because
i saw myself in you
and all I wanted was for
someone to love me the same way too…

...
I blame my naivety
for overlooking the fact that
not everyone is like me,

some want to turn their internal chaos
into something much more beautiful
and help others do the same,

while others just want to
dump it on the first person they come across,
leaving them crippled without a care in the world.

Congratulations,
you succeeded in doing just that.

My mind has become tired
from being host to
uninvited thoughts
I yearn for mental solace

where the heck
is it?

Is it vital for you to inflict pain upon me?

Do   my   tears   quench   your   thirst?

oh mom
how i wish i could tell you that
honey and garlic is not the cure
for everything....

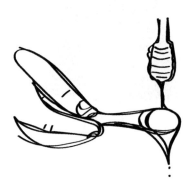

in the end
the words dried in my mouth
and the emotions seeped into my skin
awaiting another chance at escape.

~ *unable to let go*

I am
emotional instability
tear soaked pillows
i am the cut
the blade
depression
anxiety
a catastrophe
i am sugar coated lies
raw unfiltered truths

I am everything you'll never desire
but all that
truly exists.

Deda

Some days I feel like I am enough to single handedly
take on the world
other days I feel like a mere fragment of it.

Why do you always tell us to feel
when all you know is sunshine
and warm seas

do you know what it's like
to feel grey smoke entering your lungs
or overcast skies crushing your ribs

it's better to not feel and be alive
than to feel something
that will drive you to your death.

{ *sometimes not feeling is the only way to be kind to yourself* }

and what should be done
with all this anger?

when it results in self destruction
if withheld

but leads to the destruction of others
when released?

I wish for my thoughts
to roll off my tongue as easily
as they rolled into my mind

how much lighter I would feel.

Deda

I practiced what I would say
if I saw you again

how much I hate you and what you did
how I wish for your deeds to ricochet
how I even prayed for your death

and I hate
how my tongue froze in place at the
sight of you
how my blood chilled
and heart raced

it only reminded me of how
weak and helpless you make me feel
when I know I am anything but.

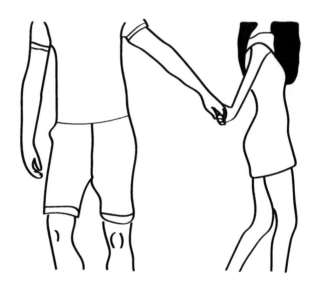

Deda

Tell me
do you recall the days our arteries
interlocked
under grey sheets
and through rays of sunshine?

when the air around us was seldom
thickened by woe
and contentment a frequent visitor

so tell me
why are we separate beings?

the state of
you and i
has bored my veins and left me
in deep depravation…

… a sense of being
stripped of purpose
branded with inadequacy
empty
without you

but tell me
is there a star a amidst
the night's darkness?
a light at the end of the tunnel?

tell me
is there even
an ounce of me
left in you?

They asked me what is life without trust,
I said, "It is a life where something you
value tremendously does not face
the constant threat of being broken."

many times we build walls to
protect ourselves from strangers,
oblivious to
or ignoring the fact that
it's the ones we love and
choose to let in that
often leave us with the
deepest wounds.

how do i tell them that i don't dislike being around them
but that the voices in my head demand enough attention

i cannot cope with hearing any more.

Once I've given you my heart
there is no gentle way of putting it back

I s

  k

   i

    p

meals because self hate is enough to keep me full.

why must my heart and mind be lifelong rivals?
it's like me hating myself.

It's hard.

being constant
sunshine

when inside you're
rainstorms
and dead trees
and withering plants.

they think I just love the color black
because when they ask I say
it's versatile and goes with everything
what I don't say is

it makes me look thinner

Deda

Today i realized how sick
i really am

that i'm probably stuck in a cycle
of self hate because
i love it

even if it drains me of energy
and nutrients
and the will to do anything
but sit

at least it keeps me skinny

and how messed up is it
that i think this way?

I workout until i'm sore

and then some more

because if i don't i feel

worthless…

…when i'm starving

and look in the mirror

i look the thinnest…..

Deda

...if i eat a sandwich
and look in said mirror
i look like i've
gained a hundred pounds

why must i be this way?

tired of hating myself
after doing what my body needs
in order to sustain itself
and survive.

Sometimes I hate myself
so much that
after every meal
i cannot help but
hold unto the toilet
and list all the things I can't
stomach about

myself.

Deda

There are times
my forgiveness says
"you're a good person but you made a mistake"

and other times it says
"I'm a good person, and I forgive you
because it is unfortunate that you're such a
despicable piece of crap."

I tore down my walls
to let you in
to let you have me
to let you have my love
my trust

but all you did was
wake me up and force me to
face reality

how am I to live in this vicious world
unprotected?

Deda

Why would you
walk into my life
only to leave?

why let me know
what it is like to
spend every day with you

and then
none at all?

Audacious of you
to think

you'd be my first choice
even after putting me second

to think i'd be
happy to have
what's left when
she's had her way
with you

i'd rather be sad and alone
than be the vacuum
to clean up what
remains
of you

- *I'd rather be alone than a second choice*

Nothing is worse than the feeling when you need all the comfort in the world but can't get it because the cause of your pain is a secret that will

have to die with you.

Our hearts have been wrecked on their journey here. We truly soiled something that could've been so beautiful. And even after all the pain and anguish, we had the nerve to call it love, the nerve to tarnish that word with something that was truly disastrous, vile and ugly.

Deda

THE
BLOOMING

When A Mind Explodes

The liquor labeled self love
left me drunk in love with
myself and sobriety was never
an option again.

Sulking in the debris of what is left of me
has gotten me nowhere

it is time I use the pieces
to build a better version
of myself.

I have had to teach myself
that my worth depends on
no one but me

for the blind may have gold
in their palm
and think
it is a mere rock.

Love yourself enough
to know that this time
will end as badly as the last

to realize that your kindness
is just a convenience to them

love yourself enough
to let go.

My mistake was expecting
to find self love within the palms
of clean hands and comfort

sometimes it is in the blood from
cuts and bruises

it was never meant to be an easy path.

They may have broken you
but you still hold the pieces
to put yourself back together
and survive.

then he loved me
through my absolute worst

and I knew
when it is the right person
there is never a
wrong time.

Deda

As I sit here
hands in lap watching
the moon tuck away
to make space for the sun
to rise

I think about how
many times beautiful things
must fade to make space
for more beautiful things

I think about us

how maybe you leaving
facilitated me
becoming who I'm
meant to be.

When I thought of love
it never looked
like dancing at 2am
or kissing in the rain
or forehead pecks

it was never in the little things

because...

… anyone can dance at 2am
but not anyone can wake at 3
and soothe you back to sleep..

… anyone can kiss you in the rain but
not all will sit in it with you
and hold you while you cry…

… anyone can place a peck
upon your forehead but
only some are willing
to bring you back when you've
wandered too far in your mind..

.. yes,
love can be found in the
little things
but only when it's found
in what matters the most.

I am forever grateful

for the ones that have left
and the lessons I've learnt

they've only made me realize
how much love and kindness
I should give the one that will
never abandon me;
myself.

Speak kind words to yourself
the world has been harsh enough towards her.

Deda

I feel like a fool
when I lay my head
on your lap and feel
like I've just reached home

when I don't feel as safe
anywhere as I do in
your arms...

95

..I feel like a fool
because I promised myself
I would never put the hammer to
destroy me in another set of hands
that weren't my own..

.. but all you've done is
help me to better myself

and for that
I want a front row seat.

I am still trying to
unlearn all that my
body whispered to me
at the darkest points of my life

no one told me it would be this
hard.

you were the gun
i turned on myself

the bullets that
bore me

leaving wounds
only self love
could aid in healing

and it did
from the inside out

it did.

I have learnt to allow
heartbreaks to restore
strength within me

weakness does not mend
broken things.

I have worked too hard
for my happiness
to take it for granted

to lay it in the palms of a
person who may walk away with it

to give it up
to someone other than
myself.

Deda

I can't get enough
of your skin under my fingertips

of your breath
on my face

your scent invading
my nostrils

of you in my head

through my veins

is this what it feels like
to drink from an
overflowing cup?

to be gloriously full
yet wanting more
all the same

is this what it feels like
when you desire someone
in their entirety

and they hand themself to you?

I do not believe in
love at first sight
but

at my first sighting of you
I knew.

Being strong is great but have you ever had a person you could be vulnerable around? Someone who never takes advantage of your lack of strength and even gives you theirs when they're in need of it themself.

and then there was a woman
who stood by
and loved me
even when she couldn't
find it within
to love herself.

We think a hard heart
will protect us from heartbreaks
but I have never seen a pillow
fall and break

it's always cold things like
ice
or hard things
like glass
that completely
shatter when hurt.

To love me you must
drown in me
a shallow heart is unable to
manage my depth

- emptiness cannot sink -

only a heart weighed with
substance can reach my core
only a heart weighed with substance

can love.

You are
a hot cup of coffee at the beginning
of a long day
and a warm shower at the end of it
the very oxygen I breathe
and the blood that flows through me

my every
want and need
personified.

It seems to me as though
the stars were crushed
as matter to mold your lips,
as if the galaxies are what
makes them full

it is the only explanation
as to why when we kiss
it feels as though the universe
is trapped between my teeth.

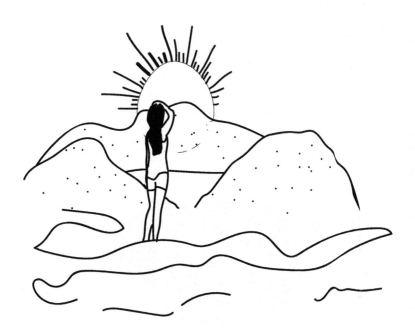

I have dreamt of
a utopia where
feeling deeply would not
destroy me

and I found it within
myself.

and when he held me
for the first time
I felt like I could finally breathe

what the heck
have I been doing all along?

I thought of you this morning
my heart didn't palpitate
i didn't cry
and even though my nails aren't
cut short my palms are free
from bruises

he touched me the same way you did
my chest did not constrict
i didn't wince
i didn't push him off
didn't feel disgusted

you have nothing over me.

the memory of you has faded
with the trauma you inflicted

i guess this is what healing feels like..

at last.

I will never
cushion the floor
beneath my heart
i want the scars
to tell the story of how i
recklessly

He says i'm as beautiful as poetry
that when he recites my name
and describes me,
the words are so saccharine,
the sweetness makes him
smile and laugh
to himself.

My heart has again
reached the edge
of the precipice
where it will fall
once again
for you.

~*can't stop falling*

Deda

I know it hurts;
what they did to you
i know you have thought
of ways to make their
deeds ricochet
so they'll know just how
agonizing it is
being on the receiving end of such cruelty

but I hope
even when the chance presents itself
that you will walk away and
be the better person.

"forever", he exhaled, as if his tongue was made
solely for the utterance of the word.. "That's what everyone said,
but when you realize how far I'm gone.." He placed a gentle kiss
upon her lips and whispered, "I will bring you back home."

Deda

Mesmerized by the way your lashes
flutter when you close your eyes

it reminds me of the state
of my heart whenever
you're around.

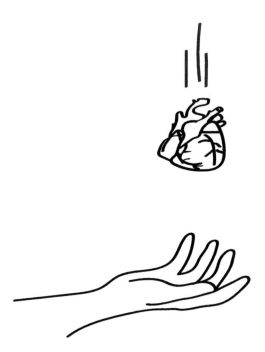

Sometimes I get lost in his eyes,
the depths of them holding me captive
as I become weak to all flowing within,
I am falling in its shackles,
losing myself in him….

…and so desperate
to not be
found.

Let me love you like you love me
like you cannot love yourself
like I need to love you

let me love you

paradox

your beauty and ugly
your strengths
and weaknesses
your whole and broken
inside through out

let my love infect your wounds
let it heal them
let me love you for you
scars
and flaws
and all.

Deda

You are still here
the real me has failed
to repulse you

the way I deep everything
a little too much
has not repelled you…

.. you are still here

after seeing me strip down the walls I've built
and stand naked before you

the mountains of their hate
has taken home to my hips
making them a bit too wide for some
but you know exactly how to hold me..

… after seeing the scars from
anxiety's tormented bites
and the blemishes in my palm
from nail digging rage
you are still here.

This must be love
is it not?

and all that came to destroy you
you overcame
and for that alone
you should be so
DAMN PROUD
of yourself.

after everything
i still hope you heal from
whatever it was that turned
you into the monster
you are.

When I have my daughter
I will feed her compliments
about how smart she is
and how beautiful her
heart is

I don't want the only
good things she hears about herself
to be about her face and body

I want her to know that is not where
her worth lies

I'm afraid she will become like
I was

obsessed with her reflection

I am afraid the toilet will
be the friend she spills her secrets to

I am afraid she'll feel
suffocating guilt for feeding
her beautiful body

Like a galaxy
and its stars
our scars

only

add

to

our

beauty.

Your beautiful eyes
shouldn't be stained by a permanent apology
it's as if you're telling the world

you're sorry for being you.

sorry for all the things you cannot control.

sorry for the emotions you are unable to
subdue.

as if when you shine in your well deserved light
you're telling the world
i'm sorry if my light was too bright
it blinded you.

At the end of the day
i concluded it
was better to be the one
with the broken heart
than to live with
the guilt of breaking
someone else's.

You can take a break from self improvement. Sometimes you can sit and be

grateful

thankful

and appreciative

of how far you've come, and bask in those feelings. Self improvement is a journey, not a laboring task, and if we don't give ourselves breaks, it will begin to feel like the latter.

God says
"After hardship comes ease."
that's what you are

my ease

you've helped me to mend myself
in ways I never thought I could be mended

completed me in a way
that makes me forget
how much has been stripped from me

taught me that
I am not my past
trauma or mistakes
but I am
whatever I think of myself

you're everything I've ever
dreamed and prayed for.

You have to think you're enough

if you're abandoned by 1000 people
you are enough

if you don't feel loved by anyone
you are enough

because the moment you think otherwise
you'll start accepting anything that makes you feel whole

and accepting anything
sometimes means
accepting the bare minimum
and you're worthy
of so much more.

forgiveness
often causes hindrance
in our "moving on"

we cannot have them up
on our backs

weighing us down

while we try to walk
away from them and
what they've done.

~ *drop the weight. forgive, and move forward freely.*

I want you to know that I am proud of you, and you should be too. After every adversity you overcame, every battle you fought solo, you are worthy of every bit of ease and happiness. Every bit of contentment. It's time to reward your body for being a wall of strength through trying times. Reward your heart for coming out stronger despite breaking many times over. Remember that hard times are inevitable, but so are good ones. You'll cry and break and feel like there is no way out sometimes, but then you'll heal and laugh and love.

Never scoff at the downfalls in life because they play a vital role in the extent of our happiness. We would never know bright days if dark ones did not exist.

~ appreciate the contrasts of life

When A Mind Explodes

If you've reached here, thank you. Thank you for reading and living vicariously through my words. For suffering with me, healing with me, and being loved with me. Thank you for your support and giving me an opportunity to feel heard.

When I finished this book, the relief I felt was both foreign and exhilarating. That's when I knew I did the right thing. I am honored to have you guys to share it with.

I hope you all are taking care of yourselves. I know it's hard but it is so worth it. Everything starts from within, so nurture yourself and the fruits of your hard work will be recognizable. Love you all.
And again,
thank you.

When A Mind Explodes

About The Author

Deda is a 21 year old woman who was born in Washington DC and raised on a small Island in the Caribbean. She has always had a love for books and when younger, found herself eager to live vicariously through each character. It was her way to escape her loud mind, until she discovered that writing does the same. When writing, she feels light hearted and heard, and only then, does her mind quiet down.

You can find her on Instagram @deda.writes
and on tiktok @_dedawrites_

Printed in Great Britain
by Amazon